THE EUGÉNIE ROCHEROLLE SERIES

Intermediate Piano Solo

It's Me, O Lord

Traditional Spirituals Arranged by Eugénie Rocherolle

T0081517

To the memory of
Esther, Mamie, Mary Jane, Susie and Winnie,
who were so much a part of my growing-up years.

ISBN-13: 978-1-4234-2004-0

HAL•LEONARD®
CORPORATION

7777 W. BLUEMOUND RD. P.O. BOX 13819 MILWAUKEE, WI 53213

In Australia Contact:
Hal Leonard Australia Pty. Ltd.
4 Lentara Court
Cheltenham, Victoria, 3192 Australia
Email: ausadmin@halleonard.com

Visit Hal Leonard Online at
www.halleonard.com

The Birth of the Spiritual Song

In 1619 a Dutch vessel landed twenty African natives at Jamestown, thus beginning the slave trade to the American colonies. It is remarkable how such an inhumane institution could lead to the birth of the uplifting and noble body of music we have come to know as African-American spirituals. These songs, which have woven themselves over time into the very fabric of American music, are a fitting testament to the enormous dignity and fortitude of the first African-Americans.

What was the initial spark that gave rise to this spontaneous collection of songs, so individual and yet so universal in their appeal? Most certainly, they were created by captive slaves who, in their helplessness and despair, found solace and hope for their survival in these songs. Many spirituals were based on biblical stories that focused on the Hebrew people and their struggle to overcome great difficulties or oppression. Frequent characters mentioned in spirituals are Moses, Ezekiel, David, and Abraham, as in the spiritual in this book "Little David, Play on Your Harp." In other instances, the spirituals speak eloquently of the sadness of the slaves' lives, such as in "Sometimes I Feel Like a Motherless Child" or "Nobody Knows the Trouble I See."

Who wrote the spirituals? Drawing on African singing traditions, it was a combination of individual talent and group response. Talented individuals, "bards," assigned to the task of making up songs, were responsible for the melody and content, but the group gave their own input by contributing the responses, or chorus part. The bard would sing a line and the chorus would respond. For example, in "Swing Low, Sweet Chariot" the chorus answers with the line "Comin' for to carry me home." This song form is known as "call-and-response." Rhythm also played an important part in spirituals and was often conveyed physically with swaying heads and bodies to express religious ecstasy, and clapping or stamping feet to express humor, or the joy of being alive.

Both emotional states, soulful longing and playful happiness, can be found in this book, in piano solo arrangements that I hope have truly captured the spirit and beauty of these wonderful songs.

—Eugénie Rocherolle
April 10, 2006

IT'S ME, O LORD

It's me, it's me, it's me, O Lord,
Standin' in the need of prayer,
It's me, it's me, it's me, O Lord,
An' I'm standin' in the need of prayer.

Tain't my mother or my father, but it's me, O Lord,
Standin' in the need of prayer,
Tain't my deacon or my leader, but it's me, O Lord,
Standin' in the need of prayer.

DEEP RIVER

Deep river, my home is over Jordan,
Deep river, Lord, I want to cross over into
    campground.
Oh, don't you want to go, to that promised
    land I know,
Deep river, my home is over Jordan,
Deep river, I want to cross over into campground.

NOBODY KNOWS THE TROUBLE I SEE

Nobody knows the trouble I see,
Nobody knows but Jesus;
Nobody knows the trouble I see,
Glory, Hallelujah!

Sometimes I'm up, sometimes I'm down,
Oh, yes, Lord;
Sometimes I'm almos' to the ground,
Oh, yes, Lord.
Although you see me goin' 'long so,
Oh, yes, Lord;
I have my trials here below,
Oh, yes, Lord.

LITTLE DAVID, PLAY ON YOUR HARP

Little David, play on your harp,
    hallelu, hallelu,
Little David, play on your harp, hallelu.

Little David was a shepherd boy,
He killed Goliath an' shouted for joy.

Joshua was the son of Nun,
He never would quit 'til his work was done.

SOMETIMES I FEEL LIKE A MOTHERLESS CHILD

Sometimes I feel like a motherless child,
Sometimes I feel like a motherless child,
Sometimes I feel like a motherless child,
A long ways from home, a long ways from home.

True believer,
A long ways from home, a long ways from home.

Sometimes I feel like I'm almos' gone,
Sometimes I feel like I'm almos' gone,
Sometimes I feel like I'm almos' gone,
Way up in the heav'nly land, way up in the
    heav'nly land.

SOMEBODY'S KNOCKIN' AT YOUR DOOR

Somebody's knockin' at your door,
Somebody's knockin' at your door,
O, sinner, why don't you answer?
Somebody's knockin' at your door.

Knocks like Jesus,
Somebody's knockin' at your door,
Knocks like Jesus,
Somebody's knockin' at your door,
O, sinner, why don't you answer?
Somebody's knockin' at your door.

Answer Jesus,
Somebody's knockin' at your door,
Answer Jesus,
Somebody's knockin' at your door,
O, sinner, why don't you answer?
Somebody's knockin' at your door.

NOBODY KNOWS THE TROUBLE I SEE (rare version)

Nobody knows the trouble I see, Lord,
Nobody knows the trouble I see,
Nobody knows the trouble I see, Lord,
Nobody knows like Jesus.

Brothers, will you pray for me?
Brothers, will you pray for me?
Brothers, will you pray for me?
An' help me to drive ol' Satan away.

Mothers, will you pray for me?
Mothers, will you pray for me?
Mothers, will you pray for me?
An' help me to drive ol' Satan away.

CAN'T YOU LIVE HUMBLE?

Can't you live humble? Praise King Jesus!
Can't you live humble to the dyin' Lamb?

Lightnin' flashes, thunders roll,
Make me think of my poor soul.
Come here Jesus, come here, please,
See me, Jesus, on my knees.

Ev'rybody, come an' see,
A man's been here from Galilee.
Came down here an' he talked to me,
Went away an' left me free.

SWING LOW, SWEET CHARIOT

Swing low, sweet chariot,
Comin' for to carry me home,
Swing low, sweet chariot,
Comin' for to carry me home.

I looked over Jordan an' what did I see,
Comin' for to carry me home,
A band of angels comin' after me,
Comin' for to carry me home.

If you get there before I do,
Comin' for to carry me home,
Tell all my friends I'm comin', too,
Comin' for to carry me home.

IT'S ME, O LORD

Traditional Spiritual
Arranged by Eugénie Rocherolle

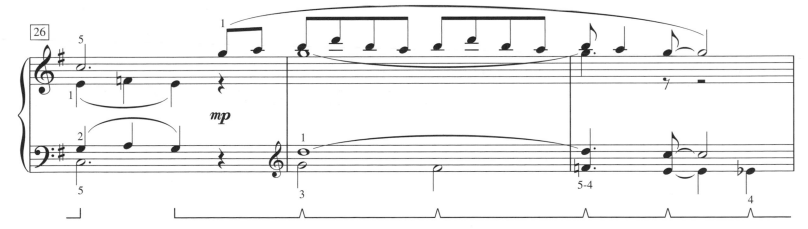

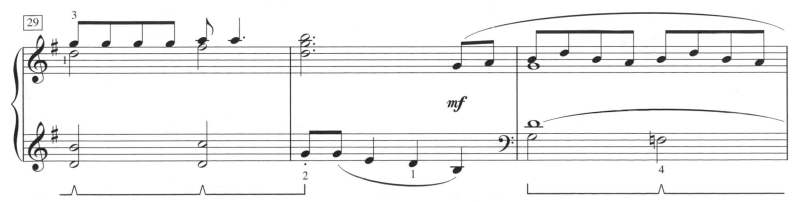

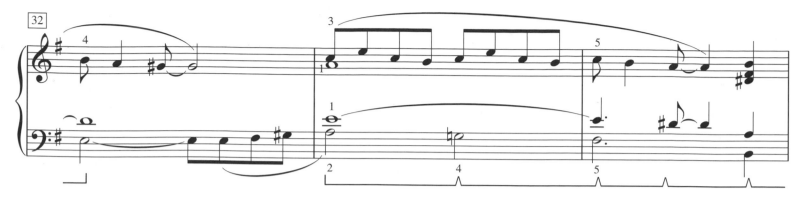

DEEP RIVER

Traditional Spiritual
Arranged by Eugénie Rocherolle

Slowly, freely ($\quarternote$ = 72)

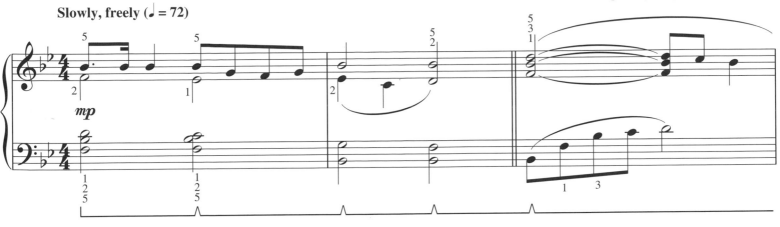

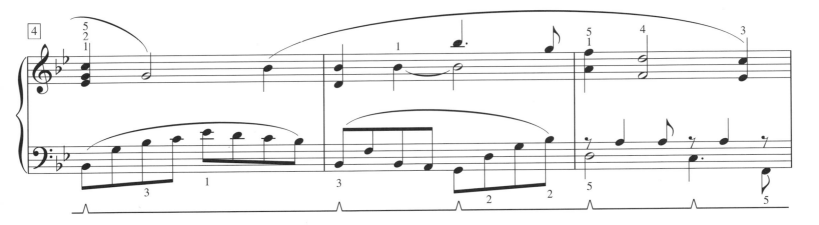

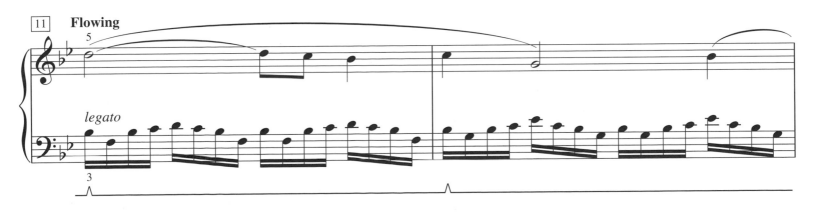

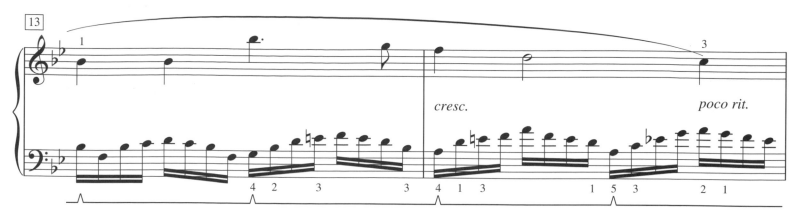

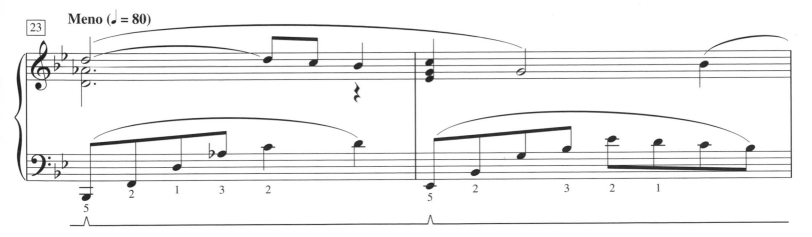

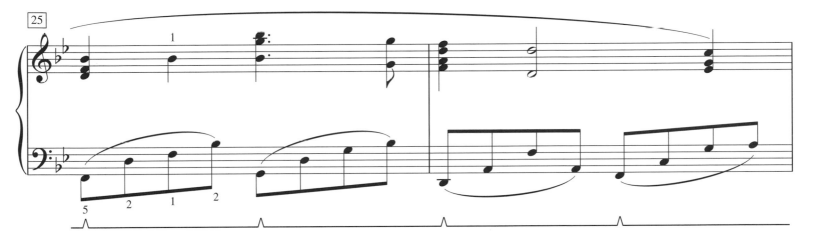

NOBODY KNOWS THE TROUBLE I SEE

Traditional Spiritual
Arranged by Eugénie Rocherolle

Slowly, freely (♩ = 69)

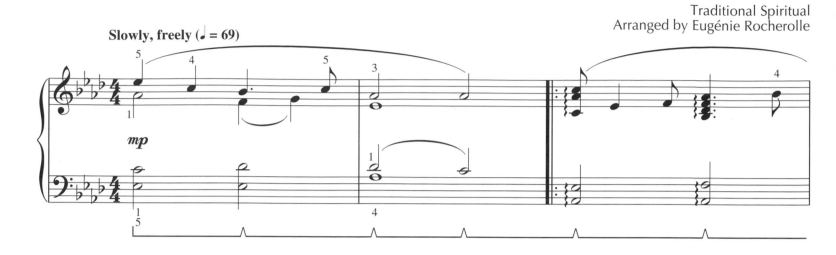

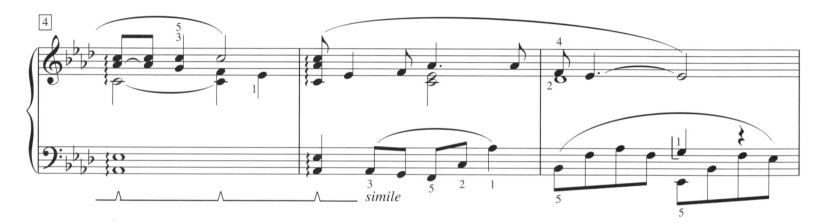

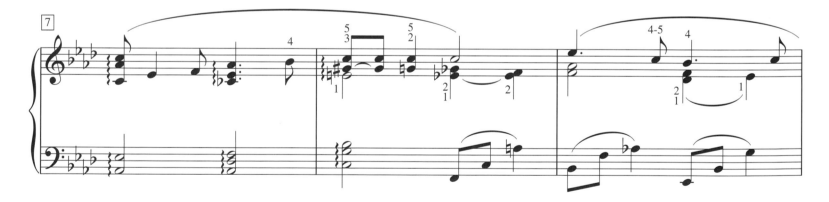

Tempo primo

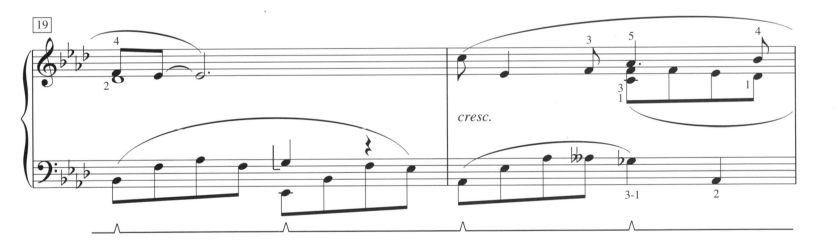

A bit slower

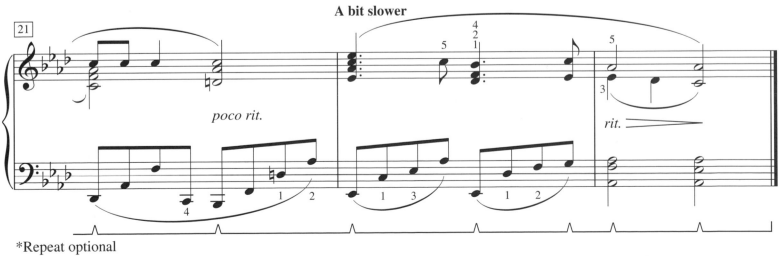

*Repeat optional

LITTLE DAVID, PLAY ON YOUR HARP

Traditional Spiritual
Arranged by Eugénie Rocherolle

Moderately fast (♩ = 126)

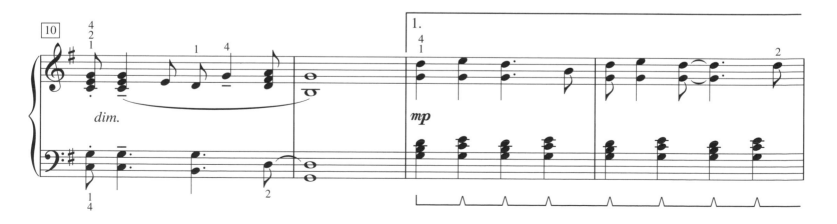

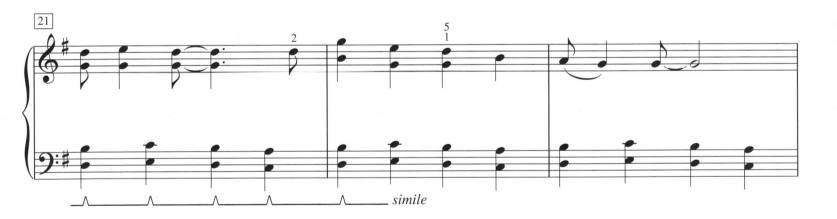

SOMETIMES I FEEL LIKE A MOTHERLESS CHILD

Traditional Spiritual
Arranged by Eugénie Rocherolle

Slowly (♩ = 69)

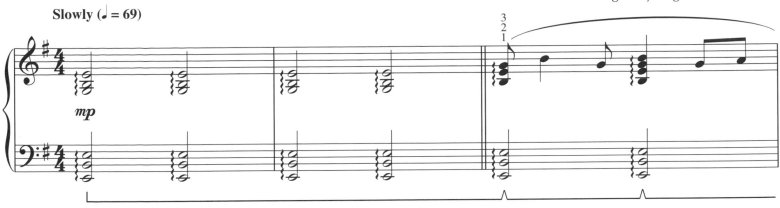

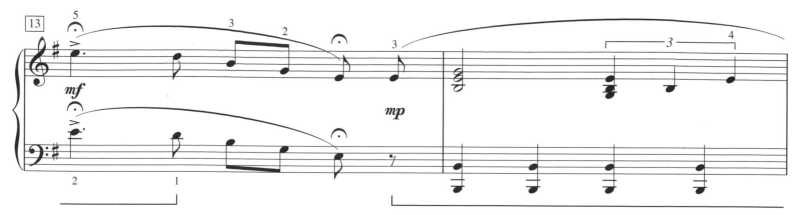

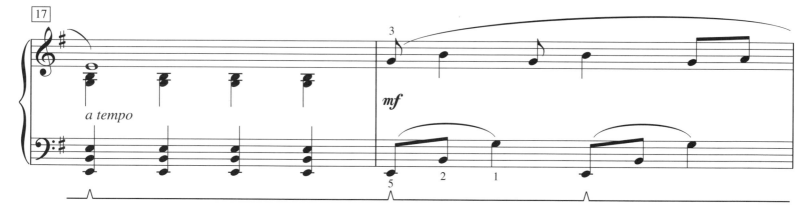

Poco mosso

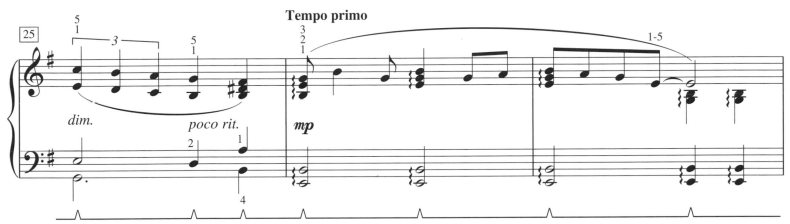

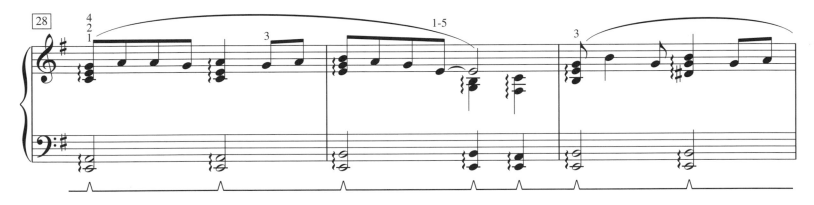

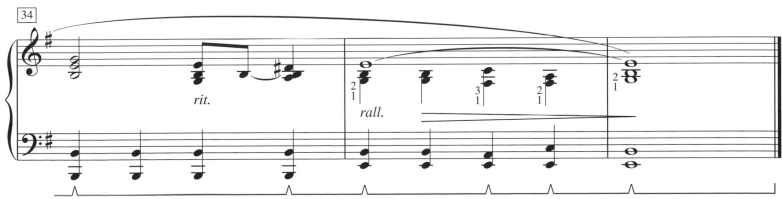

SOMEBODY'S KNOCKIN' AT YOUR DOOR

Traditional Spiritual
Arranged by Eugénie Rocherolle

Spirited ($\;$ = 84)

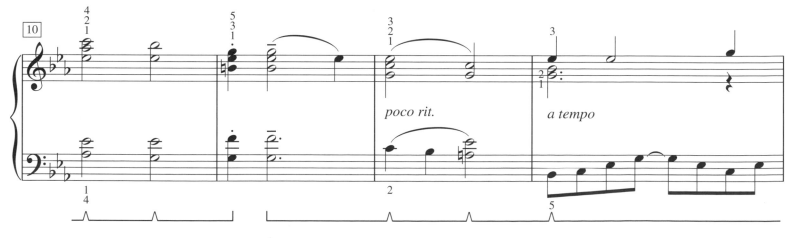

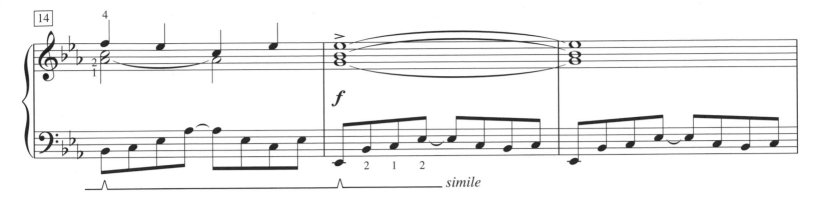

NOBODY KNOWS THE TROUBLE I SEE
(rare version)

Traditional Spiritual
Arranged by Eugénie Rocherolle

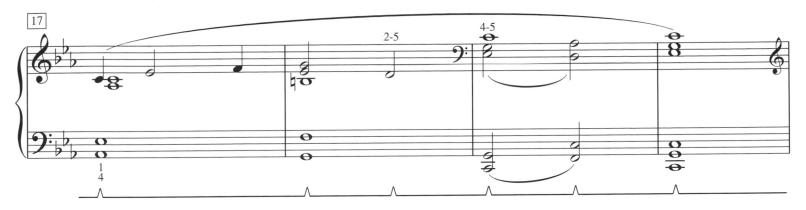

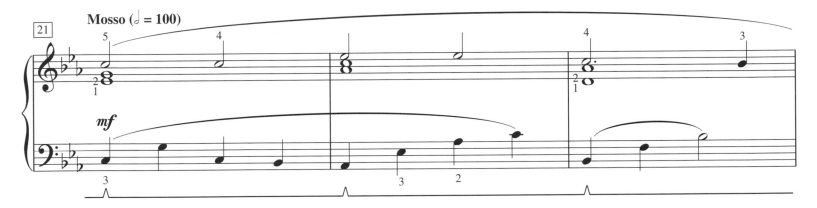

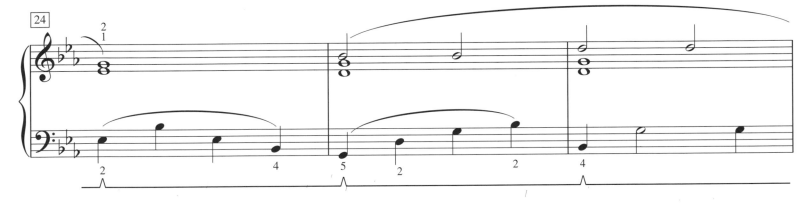

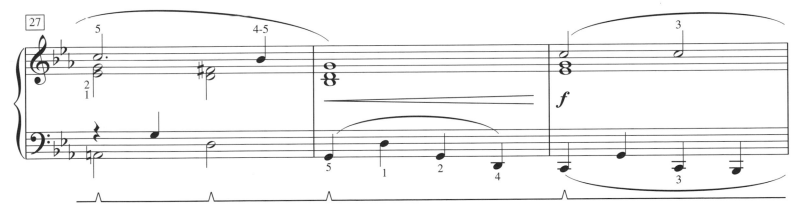

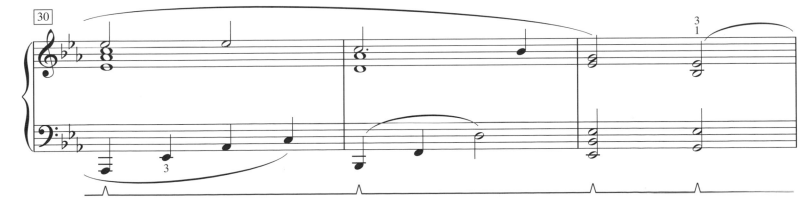

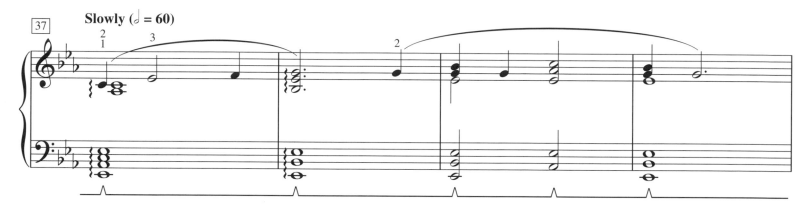

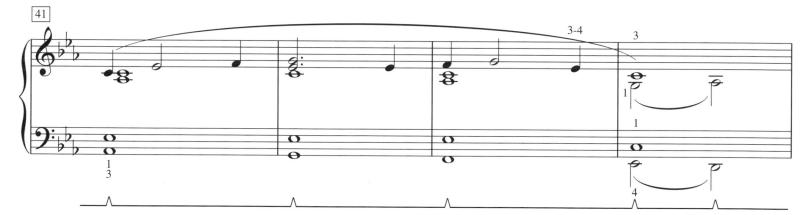

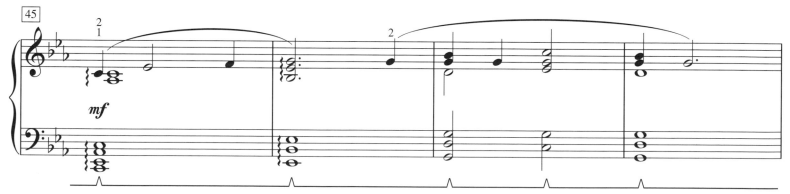

CAN'T YOU LIVE HUMBLE?

Traditional Spiritual
Arranged by Eugénie Rocherolle

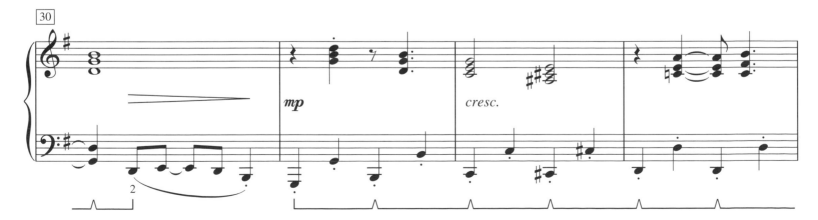

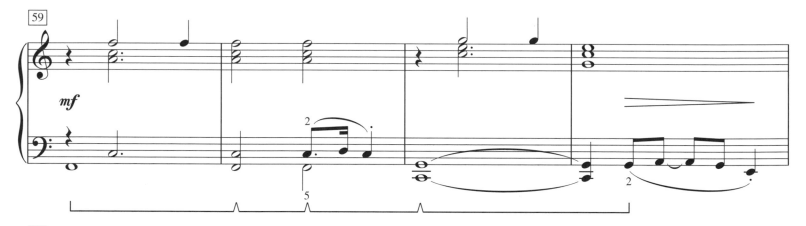

8vb

(8vb) -

(8vb) - 8vb to end

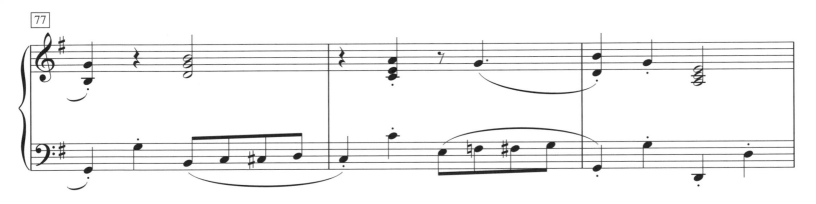

SWING LOW, SWEET CHARIOT

Traditional Spiritual
Arranged by Eugénie Rocherolle

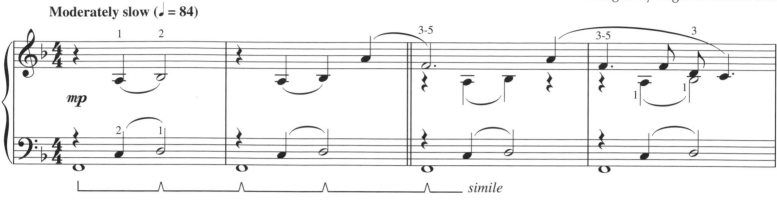

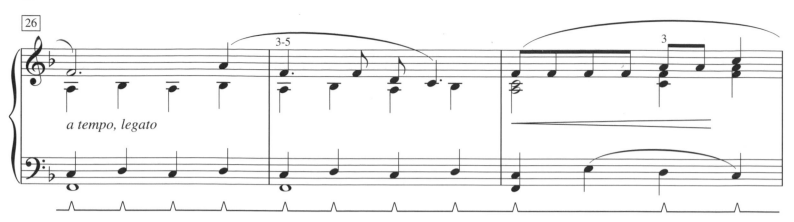

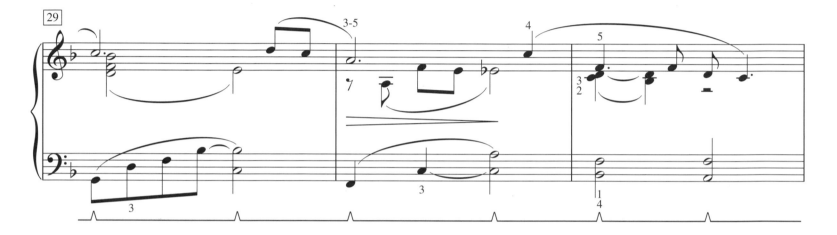

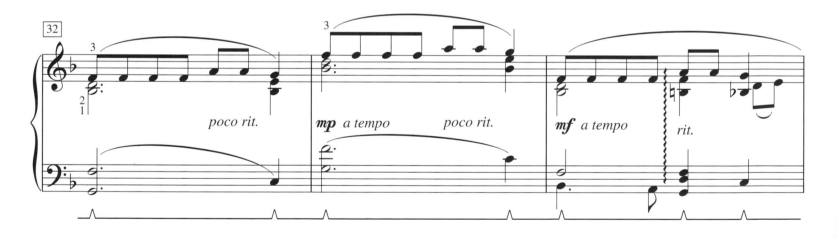